LIFE DURING THE
GREAT
CIVILIZATIONS

The Han
Dynasty

Sheila Wyborny

BLACKBIRCH®
PRESS

THOMSON
———— TM
GALE

San Diego • Detroit • New York • San Francisco • Cleveland • New Haven, Conn. • Waterville, Maine • London • Munich

THOMSON

GALE

For more information, contact
The Gale Group, Inc.
27500 Drake Rd.
Farmington Hills, MI 48331-3535
Or you can visit our Internet site at http://www.gale.com

Photo credits: see page 48.

LIBRARY OF CONGRESS CATALOGING-IN-PUBLICATION DATA

Wyborny, Sheila, 1950-
   Han Dynasty / by Sheila Wyborny.
      p. cm. — (Life during the great civilizations)
   Includes bibliographical references and index.
   Contents: Not one dynasty but two — Society and laws of the Han Dynasty — Technology, invention, and commerce — Religion and philosophy — Home and family.
      ISBN 1-56711-737-6 (hardback : alk. paper)
      1. China—Civilization—221 B.C.-960 A.D.—Juvenile literature. 2. China—Social life and customs—221 B.C.-960 A.D.—Juvenile literature. [1. China—Civilization—221 B.C.-960 A.D. 2. China —Social life and customs—221 B.C.-960 A.D.]   I. Title. II. Series.
   DS748.13.W93 2004
   931'.04—dc22   2003016279

Printed in United States
10 9 8 7 6 5 4 3 2 1

Content

Not One Dynasty but Two

The Han dynasty of China was not a single dynasty, but two. The Former, or Western, Han dynasty reigned from 206 B.C. until A.D. 8; the Later, or Eastern, Han dynasty lasted from A.D. 25 until A.D. 220. The Former Han dynasty began with a peasant revolt against the Ch'in dynasty (220 B.C.–206 B.C.), which had severely oppressed the common people while the emperor and other officials lived in luxury. Minor official Liu Pang led peasants in a revolt that successfully overthrew the Ch'in despots.

Liu Pang became the first emperor of the Former Han dynasty and established the capital city at Ch'ang-an. He worked to abolish the harsh laws that had victimized the common people and also lowered taxes and rent. Later emperors of the Western Han dynasty continued to work toward fair treatment for everyone in China, which further improved the daily lives of the common people.

As living conditions improved for the common people of China, efforts were made to improve trade as well. Emperor Wu Ti (141 B.C.–87 B.C.) sent diplomatic emissaries to the western regions of the empire, which resulted in improved trade and the exchange of knowledge. This trade route was known as the Silk Road. Prosperity and peace reigned in the Former Han dynasty for more than two hundred years until corruption, resulting from power struggles among the advisers of a succession of child emperors, weakened the empire to the point that it was ripe for revolt.

Opposite Page: Emperor Wu Ti (second from right) and other rulers of the Han dynasty led China into a time of peace, technological advancement and prosperity.

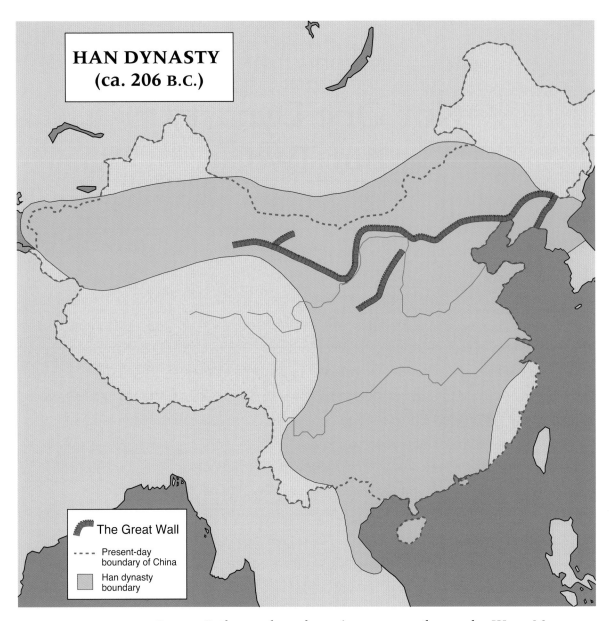

HAN DYNASTY
(ca. 206 B.C.)

The Great Wall

Present-day
boundary of China

Han dynasty
boundary

In A.D. 8, the weakened empire was overthrown by Wang Mang, a distant relative of the ruling family. Frequent wars brought his brief reign to an end in A.D. 25, when he was killed by rebels.

That same year, the Han dynasty was reestablished by another relative of the Han ruling family, Liu Hsiu, and Luoyang City became the capital of the Later Han dynasty. Liu Hsiu, like his ancestor, Liu Pang, worked to lower taxes and abolish unfair laws. He ordered workers to construct irrigation systems for farmland, which increased agricultural yield. Liu Hsiu also promoted education and ordered the release of many slaves. Liu Hsiu's successors continued to make China more prosperous by promoting the development of the bronze and textile industries. China's commerce reached new heights as the dynasty traded goods as far away as the Roman Empire.

Altogether, the Han dynasty brought peace and prosperity to the people of China for four hundred years. It was a time of creativity and technological developments. Szuma Chien, China's great historian of this time, described this period in China's history as being a time of great progress and unity.

CHAPTER ONE

Society and Laws of the Han Dynasty

The first emperor of the Han dynasty, Liu Pang, was a popular leader. Since he came from a peasant background, the people of China felt that he would be fair to all of his subjects. Indeed, he was less autocratic than previous rulers and never forgot his humble beginnings. Nevertheless, he was the most important man in China, and he understood the formidable power he wielded as emperor.

The Most Privileged

The emperor was the wealthiest and most influential man in all of Han China. He issued orders, laws, and decrees that were immediately carried out without question by state officials. His laws reached from the great palace all the way to the distant villages in the most remote regions of the empire.

Liu Pang's orders were carried out by his civil servants. Since he had been a commoner, he opened up some politically influential jobs to the common people, which created opportunities for men from middle-class families to rise in society. Civil service positions, jobs of specific ranks and responsibilities within the government, were the most sought after jobs in Han China, and with them came great respect and many rewards. Candidates for the civil service positions had to endure grueling tests that required them to memorize thousands of words in order to answer questions based on

Opposite Page: Liu Pang rose from his peasant background to become the first emperor of the Han dynasty.

Chinese history, philosophy, literature, and even appropriate table manners. They were sequestered in small rooms and carefully watched to ensure honesty. Here they wrote for two days, answering the difficult questions with brush and ink. The test was so difficult that odds against passing it were three thousand to one. Those who did pass had their names placed on a list for available jobs.

The highest-level jobs, those at the provincial and national levels, went to the students who had the highest scores. These were the most influential jobs and came with greater financial rewards, which permitted these officials to acquire large tracts of land. Those whose scores were not as good were given local civil service positions. These men enforced the law, kept the census, served as judges, supervised schools, and collected taxes within their wards.

Applicants for civil service positions took a grueling two-day exam that tested their knowledge of Chinese history, philosophy, and literature.

Commoners

Commoners included farmers, merchants, craftsmen, entertainers, and slaves. Though not as privileged as civil servants, merchants served an important role in Han society. They were a strong economic force, especially those merchants who used their profits to purchase land. Merchants, who were called the Shang class, included manufacturers, who made products to sell; traders, who traveled within and outside the empire to sell goods; and shopkeepers, who sold goods locally.

Although many merchants were honorable, hardworking people, some showed less integrity in their business dealings. For example, some would buy up crops and products to create artificial shortages and then sell them at elevated prices. Because of such behavior, Han society considered merchants to be lower in social class than farmers.

Even though Han society looked upon farming as honorable work, it was still a difficult life. During the warm seasons, farmers rose early in the morning to tend their crops. In the spring, they plowed their fields and planted seeds. On the smaller farms, family members carried water bucket by bucket from a well or a river to irrigate the fields. Later in the summer, they worked the soil with long-handled hoes, removing weeds so the crop could grow larger. In the fall, they harvested with iron sickles, implements with handles and long, curved cutting blades. In the winter, they repaired buildings and equipment.

Farmers, depicted in this brick painting, toiled throughout the year. Han society considered farming honorable work.

In the off-season, farmers were also expected to work in government labor camps to help build canals, roads, and other government construction projects.

In addition to the hard work of every season, the smaller farmers also faced the threat of being absorbed by large farming estates owned by high officials. Additionally, farmers had to produce enough crops to feed their families and pay taxes. Taxes were substantially lower in the Han dynasty than in previous times, but they still put further strain on the small farmer.

Craftsmen, who were called the Gong, were not as beleaguered as farmers. They created items ranging from ornamental but deadly weapons to delicate jewelry. Some worked in bronze and in stone, creating vessels and figures of people and animals. Bronze was also used to make mirrors, polished to a reflective sheen on one side and carved on the other. Jewelers worked with jade and other precious stones and gold to make fine jewelry for the wealthy. There were also potters,

Craftsmen and artisans passed their trades on to their sons, teaching them to make both decorative and utilitarian objects, like the vessels pictured here.

who created utilitarian and ornamental vessels. By the time of the Han dynasty, craftsmen had forged metal tools for carving, hammering, and cutting; tools far superior and longer lasting than earlier tools made of rough metals and stone.

Many craftsmen created purely ornamental pieces like this pottery figure of a musician.

Fathers passed their trades along to their sons, which led to generations of family artisans and craftsmen within the same family. At first, younger sons were expected to watch their fathers quietly and pay attention. Sometimes, they ran errands. As they learned, they were given small, simple projects. As their skills grew, so did their responsibilities, until they were considered experienced enough to work independently.

Also among the commoners were the entertainers. Like the craftsmen, singers, dancers, jugglers, acrobats, and storytellers supported themselves with their finely honed skills. Entertainers amused the wealthy and their guests during lavish feasts. Some of the wealthiest families employed their own entertainers. Emperor Wu, of the Former Han dynasty, was said to have had great admiration and affection for his personal jester, Tun-Fang Shuo.

Once, when the jester dared to help himself to a piece of meat from the emperor's table, he was called on by the emperor to explain his behavior. To defend himself, he conducted a one-sided conversation with himself: "All right now, Shuo! You have accepted the gift without waiting for the imperial command—what a breach of etiquette! You drew your sword and cut the meat—what singular daring! When you carved it up, you didn't take much—how (frugal) of you! You took it home and gave it to the little lady—how big-hearted!"[1] Fortunately for the jester, the emperor was amused, and Shuo kept the meat and his life.

Many entertainers began their training at a very young age. Occasionally, poor people sold their children to teachers who taught performing skills such as singing, dancing, and acrobatics. After several years of instruction, teachers sometimes sold these young entertainers as slaves to the wealthy. Although these young performers were little more than property of their rich owners, they fared better than other slaves.

Slaves were sold at market, like cattle. Some had been impoverished farmers who were forced to sell themselves into slavery; some had been prisoners of war. Many slaves performed manual labor, but some were taught skills and crafts to earn money for their owners. Most slaves lived the remainder of their lives in servitude, but there were a few exceptions, such as Wei Tzu-Fu, the daughter of a slave, who became an empress. Originally a servant, she gained the favor of Emperor Wu and was given the privileges of a princess. Later, she became empress. Most slaves, however, had few rights, but there was at least one law to protect them: It was against the law for masters to arbitrarily kill their slaves.

The Marketplace

The busiest part of the city was its marketplace. Drumbeats at noon signaled that the market was open for business and summoned the thousands of people who traded goods and services there. Farm families displayed their produce in large baskets on the ground, and craftsmen showcased their wares. Even barbers plied their trade in the marketplace.

This statuette depicts a fishmonger, one of the many people who traded goods and services in the bustling marketplace.

The men of the city met their friends in the wine shop, where they would buy a cup of wine and visit. Outside the shop, they might watch dancers, jugglers, and acrobats perform and drop a few coins into the entertainers' baskets to show their appreciation. They also listened to storytellers, who earned their money by telling tales. Fortune-tellers also wandered through the market and offered to tell the future of the marketers for a price. At the end of the business day, the noisy, bustling market closed and was still for the night. The next day, however, the noon drums signaled another new day's business.

Laws of the Han Dynasty

The foundation of the laws of the Han dynasty were described in simple terms by Han-era scholar Pan Ku: "In founding states and carrying on families, there are laws and regulations. A private family must not keep stores of arms, a state must not impose the death penalty arbitrarily. . . . Those who managed their duties badly were punished; those who usurped some else's office were judged guilty of a crime."[2]

Some laws applied only to specific groups of people. One group of laws, for example, applied only to merchants. They were not allowed to wear brocades, embroidery, decorated silk, linen, sackcloth, or wool.

Under the strict laws that regulated Han society, only nobles could ride in carriages, carry weapons, and wear clothing made of fine cloth.

This was because rich fabrics were reserved for the nobles, and no commoners were supposed to wear them—not even commoners who could afford to purchase them. Commoners were also not allowed to carry weapons or ride in carriages. Weapons were the domain of the military, and carriages, like fine cloth, were to be used only by nobles. The elite ranked merchants below farmers because some merchants had unethical reputations, and the nobles made every effort to keep the merchants in their place.

Punishment for serious crimes was severe. For instance, a man convicted of treason faced death. As harsh as the laws of the Han dynasty were, however, they were more lenient than those of the previous dynasty. As people had less to fear from their government, they were happier and became more productive. Freedom of thought and new ideas led to inventions and developments that increased and improved the empire and improved the daily lives of the Chinese.

Although laws and punishments for offenses were harsh during the Han dynasty, they were not as severe as those of the Ch'in dynasty.

CHAPTER TWO

Technology, Inventions, and Commerce

Thanks to more lenient laws and greater personal freedoms, some consider the Han dynasty to have been the most artistically and technologically productive of all the Chinese dynasties. Advances in agriculture, art, science, and medicine resulted from the freedom of thought fostered during this enlightened period. Commerce and trade also improved considerably.

The Silk Road

The development of the Silk Road, which contributed to the economy and expanded the empire, occurred during the reign of Emperor Wu Ti (141 B.C.–87 B.C.). In praise of this active and progressive emperor, scholar Pan Ku wrote, "He added new provinces to the number of thirty or forty, opened up new territories until he almost doubled the empire."[3]

The Silk Road was not one road but actually several trade routes throughout China and into

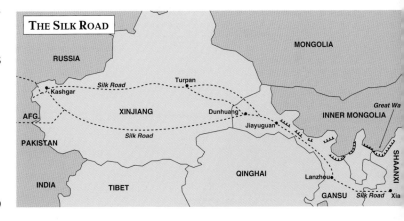

Opposite Page: Caravans traveled the Silk Road as China began to trade goods and ideas with people throughout Asia, Persia, and the farthest regions of the Roman Empire.

other countries. Wu Ti wanted to increase trade with other regions. To do this, he sent his special emissary, Chang Ch'ien, to gather information from throughout Central Asia, Persia, Arabia, and the Roman Empire. Chang Ch'ien returned with information about the culture, history, and geography of these regions. Thanks to his efforts, several trade routes were established, which made possible trade between the Han capital and these distant lands. For his efforts, Chang Ch'ien is credited as the founder of the Silk Road. The name Silk Road, however, does not adequately describe the wide range of goods that were traded.

The Silk Road expanded eastward and westward and introduced different cultures and goods throughout much of the continent. Gold and other precious metals, ivory, and precious stones were carried into China by caravan, while China exported furs, ceramics, jade, lacquerware, bronze objects, and iron. Sometimes goods were exchanged not once but several times along the way.

A photo shows remnants of the Great Wall, which Emperor Wu Ti extended to protect the caravans that traveled the northern sections of the Silk Road.

To protect the caravans of the northern trade routes, Wu Ti had the Great Wall, which was originally built in the seventh century B.C., rebuilt, reinforced, and extended. Evidence of this portion of the Great Wall's westward expansion under Wu Ti is visible today in Gansu province, where ruins of beacon towers and debris can still be seen.

History of the Great Wall

Sections of the Han Dynasty Great Wall still stand in some parts of China.

No one knows exactly when construction of the Great Wall began, but it is believed that it was originally a military fortification during the earlier Chou dynasty. In the beginning, the Great Wall was not one but several walls along the borders of China to protect it from invasion by tribes of barbarians.

The walls along the northern border were originally linked during the Ch'in dynasty, but they fell into disrepair. During the Han dynasty, however, Emperor Wu Ti had the Great Wall repaired and extended westward. Remains of the Han wall can still be seen in Dunhuang, Yumen, and Yangquan. The most complete portion of the Great Wall existing today, about 3,107 miles (5,000 kilometers) in length, was reconstructed and reinforced during the Ming dynasty.

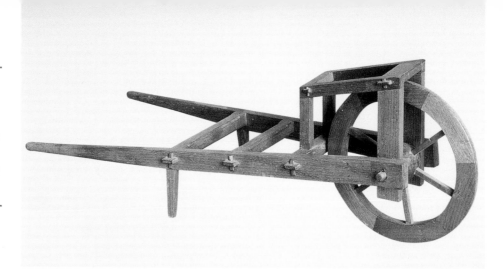

Several things were accomplished by the flourishing trade routes of the Silk Road. Wu Tu established alliances with other groups in Central Asia that permitted traders to move from place to place in relative safety. A wide variety of goods was exchanged, and this improved the economy of both Han China and the countries with which it traded. Finally, with the exchange of goods, information was shared among a variety of cultures, which broadened China's knowledge about other countries along the path of the Silk Road from Ch'ang-an all the way to the Mediterranean. This exchange of knowledge and goods and the resulting developments in science, medicine, and agriculture greatly benefited the people of the Han dynasty.

Medicine, Science, and Agriculture

The Han dynasty was responsible for a wealth of technological, artistic, and medical developments, including several innovations that greatly improved agriculture. Emperor Wu Ti decreed that the government would dig canals and ditches to manage the flow of water, which aided crop irrigation and helped control floods. The control of the flow of water enabled farmers to use water power instead of human labor to mill grain. As beneficial as these irrigation systems were to farmers, better tools made farms of the Han dynasty even more productive.

Agriculture was greatly improved due to the manufacture of iron tools. Thanks to the iron smelting process, which became widespread during the Han dynasty, farmers used metal hoes, sickles, plows, pickaxes, spades, and shovels, which helped them work the soil faster and more efficiently. These tools were much stronger than previous tools because the blast furnace produced the high temperatures needed to separate iron from iron ore in the smelting process, which resulted in strong, durable metal.

A new farm tool called the seed drill allowed farmers to sow their seeds at the correct depth. Pulled by oxen, it was made of several iron tubes that poked holes in the ground at the proper depth to plant the seed. The invention of the seed drill and the wheelbarrow, as well as the production of other iron farming tools during the Han dynasty, did not make the farmer's day any less labor intensive, but they enabled the farmer to make better use of his working hours. In addition to agriculture, creative minds of the Han dynasty made discoveries in other areas, as well.

Chang Heng (A.D. 78–A.D. 139), a government official who studied mathematics, geography, and astronomy, created two useful scientific devices. One was the seismograph, which could record earth tremors. It consisted of a vertical pole placed inside an urn that contained simple triggers. A tremor would cause the pole to tilt and activate a trigger, which released a tiny ball from one of

The seismograph, a device that records earth tremors, is just one of the many technological innovations created during the Han dynasty.

Silk

The wives of Chinese farmers made silk from the cocoons of worms that fed on the leaves of mulberry trees. First the leaves were picked from the mulberry trees and fed to the silkworms, which were kept on shelves protected from sun and rain. The worms spun cocoons, which the women soaked in hot water so the fibers could be carefully removed and woven onto reels. One delicate fiber could be over a hundred yards long. The fibers were twisted into strands on a spinner and then dyed and woven into cloth, which was pounded to make it soft, and finally ironed.

A person who told a foreigner the secret of how to make silk, one of China's most important goods, could be put to death.

The technique used to make silk was a closely guarded Chinese secret. In fact, to tell a foreigner how to make silk was a crime punishable by death. Since silk was one of the most important goods traded by the Chinese during the Han dynasty, the trade routes were collectively called the Silk Road. The Silk Road extended throughout China and into surrounding countries, and Chinese silk found its way to places as far away as Rome.

several dragon's mouths attached to the outside of the urn. The ball would fall into the mouth of one of the toads mounted on the urn's base, which indicated the direction of the tremor.

In addition to the seismograph, Chang Heng invented the armillary sphere, which measured movement in the heavens. It was made of rings that corresponded with the circular paths of planets and stars. Another area of science that experienced new developments was medicine.

Acupuncture and moxibustion, two treatments to heal illness and relieve pain, came into popular use during the Han dynasty. In acupuncture, which is still in relatively wide use in many countries today, thin needles are inserted into the skin at certain points along the body. In moxibustion, special herbs are burnt directly onto the skin at specific points on the body. Another medical discovery of the Han dynasty was an anesthetic made from the peony plant in about A.D.

207 by physician Hua Tuo. Before anesthesia, many people died from shock during surgery due to pain.

Medical and technological developments during the Han dynasty greatly improved the quality of life. Farms were more productive, earthquakes could be detected from their first tremors, and medical treatments helped improve peoples' health. This was a productive era for science and medicine, and it was an equally productive time for the arts as well.

The Arts

Chinese of the Han dynasty prized lacquerware, like this ornate basket found in a tomb from that period, over bronze.

Freedom of thought during the Han dynasty encouraged creativity, which led to several developments in the arts. Lacquerware—glossy, decorative vessels, boxes, furniture, and musical instruments—was produced in small factories during the Han dynasty. Artisans painted coats of lacquer, the resin of the sumac tree, onto a thin wooden object, allowed the layer to dry, and painted it again. This procedure was repeated many times until the object had a hard surface.

Powdered minerals were added to the lacquer to give it color. During the Han dynasty, lacquerware was more valuable than bronze.

Another process developed during the Han dynasty was papermaking. Before the development of the papermaking process, writing was done on silk, which was so expensive that few people could afford written materials. In about A.D. 105, court official Ts'ai Lun developed a papermaking process. He first broke mulberry bark into fibers and pounded it into sheets. Later, he improved on his original process. He discovered that adding ground hemp, rags, and old fishnets strengthened the paper. In addition to writing, the paper was also used for painting, umbrellas, fans, and window coverings. While the efforts of Ts'ai Lun and other innovative people of the Han dynasty changed how people of this period lived, religion and the teachings of one philosopher influenced the beliefs of the people of Han China.

Ts'ai Lun (right) developed a process for making paper (left). Paper soon began to replace silk, a much more expensive writing material.

CHAPTER THREE

Religion and Philosophy

The beliefs of the people of the Han dynasty were a mixture of philosophy and several religions. Based on Confucianism, Buddhism, and Taoism, their beliefs combined harmony with nature, meditation, and ancestor worship into a lifestyle of balance and order. They believed that if people behaved properly, they would be in harmony with nature.

Followers of Taoism believed that people should follow universal laws, or laws of nature, rather than human laws. "The Way," as they called their lifestyle, was characterized by living a simple life, keeping close to nature, and meditating. They also believed in making sacrifices to the spirits of the mountains and trees, so these spirits would use their magic in favor of the Taoists. The Taoists also used prayer and diet in their quest for eternal youth. The search for eternal youth became a major focus for Taoists during the Han dynasty, and some Taoist masters claimed that they could actually prolong life forever.

In some ways, such as the practice of meditation and self discipline, the teachings of Buddhism were similar to Taoism. Buddhism came to China from India as a result of the trade between the two regions on the Silk Road during the Han dynasty. The religion began quietly in China but grew steadily. Buddhism taught that in order to attain enlightenment, a person should live a spiritual life rather than be overly ambitious or seek many worldly possessions.

Opposite Page: The teachings of Confucius, depicted in this colorful scroll painting, guided every aspect of Han life, from government to personal relationships.

Buddhism teaches that a person should not be overly ambitious or seek worldly possessions, but should live a spiritual life.

The philosophy of Confucius, however, taught that happiness and an orderly life were achieved through obedience to authority. Confucius was a civil servant and teacher who lived before the Han dynasty, but his teachings set the standard for Han government. His words, as recorded in five books, formed the basis of civil service training. According to Confucius: "All six arts help govern. The Book of Rites helps to regulate men, the Book of Music brings about harmony, the Book of Documents records incidents, the Book of Song expresses emotions, the Book of Change reveals supernatural influence, and Spring and Autumn annals show what is right."[4]

According to Confucianism, rulers should set good examples for their subjects and be fair and benevolent toward them. In turn, the people should be obedient and loyal to authority. In addition, Confucianism taught that people preparing for a career in government should be trained to be fair and honest. Confucianism also taught that the government should be conscientious regarding the welfare of common people.

Religion and philosophy affected every part of life in the Han dynasty. Everything from the role of government to the conduct of

Confucius

Also known as K'ung Fu-tzu, Confucius was born about 551 B.C. in eastern China. His family was not wealthy, so Confucius had to earn a living. Even though he was mostly self-educated, he became a teacher. Confucius was concerned about the plight of the common people. He also sought social change by nonviolent means.

Confucius believed that good government depended on fair and honest civil servants.

Confucius wanted to change and improve the government. He proposed that the people who would one day work for the government be trained in the skills they would need to be good civil servants. He also wanted them taught to be fair and honest.

Confucius left no writings, but his sayings were collected by his students and published in books. One book, *Analects*, contained thoughts on establishing a fair and orderly society and described dominant and subservient roles. These teachings served as the basis for civil service training of the Han dynasty.

personal relationships were guided by religion and the teachings of Confucius. The people of the Han dynasty celebrated their beliefs with ceremonies and festivals that honored their ancestors and their gods.

Rituals and Celebrations

The people of Han China held public religious festivals led by priests to ensure abundant crops and to honor the spirits when they had a good harvest. The festival in which they thanked the spirits for a good harvest was called the Grand Festival in Honor of Spirits Who Are to be Sought Out. Several spirits were honored, including the spirits of tigers, which kept wild hogs out of the farmers' fields, and the spirits of cats, which killed the rats that could destroy the grain. Adults and children wore cat and tiger costumes during the festival.

The teachings of Confucius (second from left in this Han rubbing) explain that obedience to authority leads to a happy, orderly life.

Families also held private ceremonies in their homes. They built household altars to worship the spirits of their ancestors, and they held ceremonies on the anniversaries of the births and deaths of their ancestors. To honor their ancestors, they offered them food and drink and prayed to them. Names of deceased family members were written on tablets, which were placed on the altar. Bowls of food and incense

were placed in front of the tablets. All members of the family took their turn at the household altar, where they knelt on the floor three times and touched their foreheads to the floor nine times.

Burial Rites

Rituals and ceremonies played a big part in the lives of the people of Han China, and one of the most important rituals was preparing deceased loved ones for the afterlife. In most cases, the dead were treated with great respect by the Chinese people, but the type of burial depended on the deceased person's station in life. Slaves and laborers were buried in rough pits; some of the slaves still wore their chains. Sometimes a brick on which their skills and date of death were inscribed were buried with laborers. Although families provided what they could to see their loved ones into the next world, the poor went to humble graves and were interred in cheap coffins with a few pots for their grave goods, which were foods and other items buried with the deceased to help them in the afterlife. The rich, however, went to

Buddhism

Siddartha, an Indian prince, founded Buddhism, which spread to China during the Han dynasty.

Buddhism came to China from India during the Han dynasty by way of traders along the Silk Road. It was founded by an Indian prince, Siddartha, in about 528 B.C. Buddha means "Enlightened One."

According to the history of this religion, Prince Siddartha, although raised in luxury, decided that extremes of wealth and poverty were equally wrong. He taught that salvation came from following a middle path, not one of selfishness, extreme ambition, or the collection of many possessions. Buddhism is still practiced by many people today.

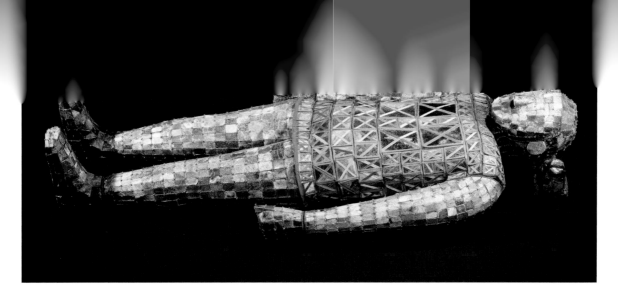

great expense to provide lavish final resting places and grave goods for their deceased family members.

Aristocrats of the Han dynasty were buried in horizontal underground chambers that were decorated to resemble the homes of the living and outfitted with elaborate grave goods, food, and drink. Grave goods included models of carriages, people, and horses, some of which were made of jade or cast in bronze.

The deceased were dressed in elaborate burial suits, sometimes made from precious metals and stones. The one made for Prince Liu Sheng, son of a Han emperor, included a burial suit and mask made of 2,498 pieces of jade that were linked together with gold wire. The nobles of Han China believed that elaborate suits would preserve the body. Twentieth-century excavations, however, revealed perfectly preserved burial suits but bodies that had turned to dust.

Religion and Confucianism influenced the lives of the people of Han China from birth to death. Rituals and ceremonies were a part of their daily lives, and order, obedience, and honesty, foundations of the Confucian philosophy, also influenced family relationships.

A Han princess was buried in this jade suit. Han nobles believed that burial suits would preserve their bodies after death.

CHAPTER FOUR

Home and Family

Rich or poor, large or small, families of the Han dynasty followed the principles of honor and obedience. Parents were supposed to set a good example, and children were expected to obey and respect their parents. In the words of Han scholar Pan Ku: "A true filial son is one who is careful to abide by his father's wishes and to bring to completion what his father began."[5]

Homes

Home and family were important elements in the social structure of Han society, and family members valued their time together. Wealthy families led comfortable lives, wore fine clothing, and lived in large, elaborate, beautifully decorated homes. Visitors to a typical upper-class home entered by a main gate that led to the first courtyard. If the visitors were tradesmen, this is where they were received. Family members, however, proceeded to a second, inner courtyard, surrounded by main rooms where the immediate family lived and side rooms for other relatives who lived in the household. The house had two sitting rooms, one for the wife and a larger one for the husband, as well as private baths. The house contained richly carved furniture, and woolen rugs or woven mats covered the floor. Privacy was provided by elaborately decorated screens. The kitchen and servants' quarters were located behind this main building.

Opposite Page: Both rich and poor families
followed principles that required children to
respect and obey their parents unconditionally.

One especially elaborate home was described by historian Szuma Chien: "The front palace . . . built first . . . was five hundred paces from east to west, and five hundred paces from south to north. The terraces above could seat ten thousand. . . . A labor force of more than seven hundred thousand was drafted to build the palace."[6]

Homes of the poor, however, were very basic. Privacy was not an issue; in fact, there was barely room for all members of the family. Because peasants lived very simply and spent their days tending crops and doing manual labor, they had neither spare time nor money for luxuries. The homes of the poor were thatch-roofed, mud-plastered huts. For insulation in the winter, the peasants placed hemp curtains

Wealthy families lived in large homes with many beautifully decorated rooms.

over the windows and huddled under quilts. Their beds were rush mats, and pillows were made from wood or pottery. For bathrooms, they made do with communal latrines and drains.

Food

In most families, whether rich or poor, men and women usually had their meals together. The foods eaten by the rich and the poor, however, were as different as their homes. In the homes of the wealthy, guests sat on rich rugs or plush cushions and dined on such delicacies as dog cutlets, bear's paw, and panther's breast. They had variety in their meals and also ate pork, mutton, fish, quail, and baby goat. Favorite vegetables were bamboo shoots and lotus root accompanied by fine grape wines, which were first produced in China during the Han dynasty. Fruit was usually served at the end of the meal. These large, elaborate meals were served in fine porcelain bowls and plates with chopsticks made from bamboo, wood, or ivory.

Peasants' meals were not so elaborate. They had wheat and millet cakes, rice, beans, leeks, turnips, and cabbage. Sometimes, they also ate peaches, melons, and plums. For special occasions, such as weddings or birthdays of elderly family members, they had a bit of pork, chicken, or beef with their meals, accompanied by alcoholic beverages made from fermented millet or rice. Sometimes, however, the poor did not have enough to eat. In large families, there sometimes was not enough food to go around. Survival was a full-time job for poor families, and all family members had to work together just to get by.

Roles of Family Members

The wealthy enjoyed elaborate meals that included favorite vegetables like bamboo shoots and lotus roots (pictured).

In peasant families, children learned the work of their parents. Farm children, for example, learned to tend animals and plant and raise crops. The children had to work along with their parents if the farm and the family were to survive. Since some farmwork was too physically demanding for smaller girls, the more sons a family had, the more successful their farm was.

Boys were more highly valued than girls in rich families as well, because men were considered to be superior to women throughout Han society, and people believed that parents who had sons would become gods in the afterlife. Boys and girls were raised together and played together until they were teenagers, but they were then separated and trained in the roles they would follow for life. When a girl turned fifteen, her hair was pinned up in a ceremony that meant she was now considered a grown woman. Boys had a ceremony at about twenty years of age called a capping ceremony. At this time, the boy's hairstyle was changed from the childhood style, worn in two plugs of hair on each side of his head, to a bun on top of his head. Next, a cap was placed on his head, signifying that he was now a man and could no longer wear his hair uncovered in public.

As a part of these ceremonies, which initiated boys and girls into adulthood, young people were given adult names to replace their

At the age of fifteen, a girl would begin to wear her hair pinned up to indicate that she had reached adulthood.

Leisure Time and Celebrations

Acrobats (pictured) and other traveling performers entertained crowds at Han dynasty celebrations.

Most leisure-time activities were enjoyed by the wealthy, but although the poor had little free time, they occasionally found time for a little fun. Both rich and poor enjoyed kite flying and games of shuttlecock, which is similar to badminton. They also liked to watch performances of traveling troupes of entertainers. In the cities, parks were favorite places for taking a stroll or having a picnic.

The wealthy had large, noisy parties. They also hunted for sport. Some of the wealthy even had their own troupes of entertainers for their own enjoyment and the amusement of their guests.

Fireworks were popular among all classes in Han society. During the New Year's Day festival, when children would dress in their best clothes and share sweets with family and friends, fireworks were exploded in front of homes to ward off evil spirits. Another time for celebration was the fall festival, which was held on the night that the moon was supposed to be at its brightest. On this night, children hung brightly colored lanterns in the courtyards of their homes. These festivals and celebrations were fun for both the adults and children of the Han dynasty.

childhood names. Now recognized as adults in Han society, the young men and women took on adult responsibilities. The young men were ready to study for civil service jobs or enter the military, and the young women prepared for their adult roles by learning household skills. They were ready to marry and start their own families.

Most Chinese households, whether of nobles or commoners, were multigenerational. Grandparents usually lived in the homes of their adult children and their grandchildren. From their earliest years, children were taught to respect and honor their elders and to learn from them.

These strong family relationships, together with the inventions and advancements in agriculture and successful trade, resulted in what some historians call the most productive of all the Chinese dynasties. The rich legacy of the Han dynasty, begun by a peasant emperor, set new standards in democracy, art, medicine, and science unequaled by any other civilization of its era.

Notes

Chapter 1: Society and Laws of the Han Dynasty

1. Quoted in Burton Watson, trans., *Courtier and Commoner in Ancient China: Selections from the History of the Former Han* by Pan Ku. New York: Columbia Press, 1974, p. 83.
2. Quoted in Watson, *Courtier and Commoner in Ancient China,* p. 222.

Chapter 2: Technology, Inventions, and Commerce

3. Quoted in Watson, *Courtier and Commoner in Ancient China,* p. 56.

Chapter 3: Religion and Philosophy

4. Quoted in Szuma Chien, *Records of the Historian.* Peking, China: 1979, p. 403.

Chapter 4: Home and Family

5. Quoted in Watson, *Courtier and Commoner in Ancient China,* p. 275.
6. Chien, *Records of the Historian,* p. 179.

Glossary

alliance: An association of nations or groups to promote common interests.

ancestor: Someone from whom a person is descended.

anesthesia: A drug that causes loss of sensation in the body.

autocratic: Ruling with unlimited power.

barbarian: A person of a primitive civilization.

brocade: A rich fabric woven with a raised design.

dynasty: A succession of rulers from the same family.

emissary: An agent or representative sent on a mission to promote the interests of a group or a country.

lacquerware: Furniture, vases, or other decorative items made by painting many layers of a tree resin onto an object to create a hard, shiny surface.

seismograph: An instrument for detecting the direction and intensity of earth tremors.

smelting: Using furnaces with extremely high temperatures to melt ores and separate the metal content.

For More Information

Books

Amy Allison, *Life in Ancient China*. San Diego, CA: Lucent Books, 2001.

Leonard Everett Fishr, *The Great Wall of China*. New York: Macmillan, 1986.

John Hay, *Ancient China*. New York: Henry Zwalck, 1973.

Penelope Hughes-Stanton, *An Ancient Chinese Town*. New York: Warwick Press, 1986.

Lai Po Kan, *The Ancient Chinese*. Morristown, NJ: Silver Burdett, 1985.

Theodore Rowland-Entwhistle, *Confucius and Ancient China*. New York: Boatwright Press, 1987.

Websites

Chinaknowledge (www.chinaknowledge.de). This website describes the growth of the Western, or Former, Han dynasty and of the Eastern, or Later, Han dynasty with links to relevant information.

The Silk Road (www.ess.uci.edu). This website describes the history of the development, height, and decline of the Silk Road.

Index

Picture Credits

About the Author

Sheila Wyborny and her husband, Wendell, live in Houston, Texas. They are in the process of building a home at an airport in a nearby community so they can park their aircraft, a Cessna 170B, in their backyard.